Theodore's Chinese Adventures

Ni hao (hello) everyone. I'm really excited to share my amazing adventure to **China** with you. The people, culture and history are different to many other countries. China also has many varied landscapes including deserts, mountains and rich green farmland.

Here are some more interesting things about China:

- China has the **biggest** population in the world (nearly 1.4 billion people).
- It is called the People's Republic of China.
- The capital is **Beijing** and the most populated city is Shanghai.
- **Red** is the symbol for **happiness**.

The main language in China is **Mandarin**, but there are many other languages.

Mandarin is written in beautiful characters that children learn from an early age. There are thousands of characters that are learned over a life time. Writing each character is like drawing a tiny picture for example:

Hello – 你好

I like to learn a few words when I travel to be friendly and polite. Maybe you can try to say some of these.

English	Chinese	Saying It
Hello	ni hao	nee how
Goodbye	zai jian	zai jean
Thank you	xie–xie	shea shea
How are you?	ni hao ma	nee how mah?
Please	qing	ching
Yes	shi	shr
No	bu shi	boo shr

The **Great Wall of China** is probably the most famous tourist attraction in China. It winds through the countryside and across hills and mountains all the way from the Korean border into the Gobi desert. The wall is 8,850 km/5,500 miles long.

If you go there you will be able to say that you walked along the **longest wall** in the world.

In **1999** The Great Wall Marathon started. It has grown into a major event and each year many travel to run this beautiful and difficult course.

Kung Fu is one of the oldest forms of martial arts. Monks have been practicing Kung Fu for hundreds of years at the Shaolin Monastery.

The term Kung Fu actually means 'acquired skill'. There is a lot of hard work and training involved in getting good at this martial art.

There are some famous actors and films that feature Kung Fu. They include actors such as Bruce Lee and Jackie Chan. Kung Fu Panda is a really funny kids movie.

Have you seen any of these?

Table tennis is one of the most popular sports in China. It was declared the national sport in the 1950's by Chairman Mao.

The Chinese win many world and Olympic championships and children who show potential in the game go to academies to practice table tennis. It is played in many places including schools and outdoor parks.

Other popular sports include badminton, basketball, volleyball and soccer.

Chinese food is really delicious. They use lots of fish, meat and vegetables with many herbs and spices. Rice is eaten with most meals and is a staple food of the country. Rice is also one of the major crops grown in China.

There were a few foods that were so yummy I wanted to share them with you.

Dumplings – little pastry parcels with delicious fillings

Hot Pot – meat, fish or vegetables simmered in a broth

It's also great fun to finish the meal with a crunchy biscuit called a **fortune cookie**. It has a little piece of paper with your fortune written on the inside when you break it open.

Did you know that **chopsticks** were created in China about **5,000** years ago? It is believed that the first chopsticks were used for cooking and made from twigs.
How 's that for a really fun fact?

Traditionally, Chinese chopsticks are made from wood or bamboo. If you eat with chopsticks, it is poor etiquette to spear your food or tap your chopsticks on the edge of your bowl.

Have you ever tried using them?

Robot restaurants have popped up in China in the last few years. They are lots of fun, tourists and locals love the idea of being served by a robot.

In some restaurants, they **greet** you at the door, **take your order** and **deliver** food to the table. How awesome!

The robots make beeping sounds and have been designed to understand about 40 everyday sentences. They can work about five hours before they have to be recharged and have sensors which tell them where they are going.

I hope you get a chance to eat at a robot restaurant.

The **Big Buddha** or Tian Tan Buddha is in **Hong Kong**. It is a really big bronze statue that was built in 1933 and is the second largest sitting Buddha in the world.

The Buddha stands for the peaceful relationship between man and nature as well as people and faith, so has a really important message for all of us.

My little legs climbed over **260** steps to reach the top and I lost count of the steps as I got closer to the top.
 (You can get a cable car to the top if you don't want to walk).

Hong Kong is hard to beat as a shopping destination. There is something for everyone and somewhere to go and shop.

There are designer shops and exclusive labels, as well as silk products and artwork to buy.

Two great street markets are Kowloon Street and the Temple Street night market.

The landmark called 'Central' is one of the oldest shopping malls in Hong Kong.

Hangzhou is a historical and cultural city that is about an hour away from Shanghai on the **bullet train**.

West Lake is one of the most beautiful places in china and was listed as a World Heritage Site in 2011. It is also the symbol of Hangzhou.

Hangzhou is known as the 'Capital of Tea in China'. If you love tea, there are tea tours that you can do here.

Hangzhou is also famous for its **silk**. There are many great souvenirs to buy and take home with you.

One of the most amazing things to see in China is the Terracotta Army which is in Xi'an, central China. It was discovered in 1976 by farmers who were digging a well in the area.

There are about 8,000 life sized sculptures of soldiers, horses and other figures.

The soldiers took around 40 years to build. They were built to protect the first Emperor, Emperor Qin in the afterlife. There are three large pits and a museum to explore.

The **giant panda** is un 'bear 'ably cute (maybe even cuter than me). They live in the mountains of central China and are on the endangered species list as there are not many left in the wild.

There are three main panda reserves around the Chengdu area. It 's best to see the pandas early in the morning when they are most active and playful. They get pretty lazy and do lots of relaxing when it 's hot.

The zoos in Beijing and Shanghai also have pandas, if you can 't go to Chengdu.

A giant panda can eat up to 40pds/18kgs of bamboo in one day!

Shadow puppetry, also known as shadow play, is a Chinese folk art that has been popular in China for thousands of years. The puppets were first made of paper, then later from the leather of animals. That's why their Chinese name is **pi ying**, meaning **shadows of leather**.

The puppet shows originated in **Xi'an** and might be the best place to see a show, however, there are puppet theatres throughout China.

Here is a really interesting fact for you. Dragons are seen as symbols of **power** and **good luck** in China.

A favorite destination for many tourists is the **Forbidden City in Beijing**. It is always a very busy place to see so its best to go mid-week if you can.

The palace was built between **1406 and 1420 AD** (that's really, really old) and is now a museum. More than 20 emperors have lived in the palace.

The palace has over **9000** rooms filled with ancient artifacts. The grounds are around **250** acres, (that's huge) and it's the largest ancient palace in the world.

Yellow Mountain is in **Huangshan City**. It is a UNESCO World Heritage Site and one of China's major tourist destinations.

The area is so beautiful that it takes your breath away. There are amazing **sunrises** and **sunsets** and really odd shaped **granite peaks** surrounded by a sea of clouds. You see ancient **dwarf pines** that grow all over the rocks. If that does not excite you enough, there are also **hot springs** and **waterfalls** to visit. Many medicinal herbs can be found at Huangshan Mountain.

If you go there, you will enjoy the beauty of nature and an experience that you will never forget.

One fun way to enjoy exploring the sights is to take a rickshaw ride.

These old-fashioned bikes used to travel through the hutongs (narrow lanes) and are a fun way to get around in many Chinese cities. They are easily found around tourist sites, but you have to do a bit of bargaining if you don't want to be overcharged.

This is where my Chinese adventure ends. I hope you loved sharing mine and learned about china along the way.

Zai jian from Theodore.

Theodore's Adventure Series

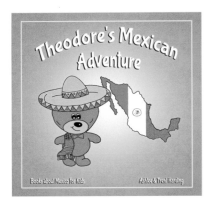

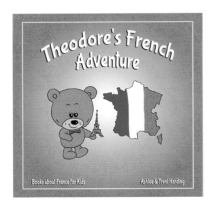

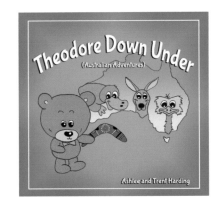

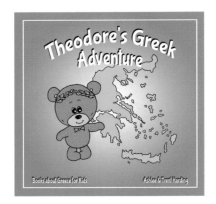

Also...

Other educational books written by us

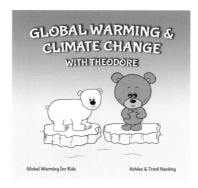

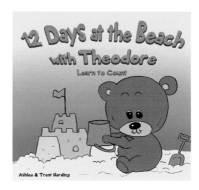

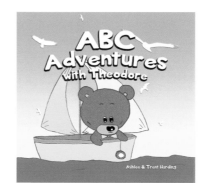

Made in United States
Troutdale, OR
05/04/2025

31105061R00024